YOUR KNOWLEDGE HAS VALUE

- We will publish your bachelor's and master's thesis, essays and papers

- Your own eBook and book - sold worldwide in all relevant shops

- Earn money with each sale

Upload your text at www.GRIN.com
and publish for free

The Conflict Between Reason and Emotion. Analysing Philip Larkin's Poem 'No Road'

Ana Colton-Sonnenberg

Bibliographic information published by the German National Library:

The German National Library lists this publication in the National Bibliography; detailed bibliographic data are available on the Internet at http://dnb.dnb.de.

ISBN: 9783668180895
This book is also available as an ebook.

© GRIN Publishing GmbH
Trappentreustraße 1
80339 München

All rights reserved

Print and binding: Books on Demand GmbH, Norderstedt, Germany
Printed on acid-free paper from responsible sources.

The present work has been carefully prepared. Nevertheless, authors and publishers do not incur liability for the correctness of information, notes, links and advice as well as any printing errors.

GRIN web shop: https://www.grin.com/document/71208

Universität Paderborn
CLC-Advanced 1

Essay by

Ana Colton-Sonnenberg

"No Road"

Concerning:
Philip Larkin's "No Road"

The title of Philip Larkin's "No Road" already introduces the reader to the gloomy atmosphere prevailing in the poem. In it, the persona reflects the process of letting-go of his former partner after the mutually agreed end of their relationship. Despite the strong feelings that both partners still seem to have for each other, it is not possible for them to stay together. What the poem is essentially about is the eternal human conflict between ratio and emotion. Central to this topic is the suffering caused by this antagonism. The principle devices used to communicate the theme of suffering in the poem are the narrative framework and the language. The latter is full of imagery, simile, alliteration, enjambment, and litotes. How these devices work in the communication will be discussed in the following.

Instead of presenting the subject matter in a direct, factual way, the author of the poem has chosen to embed it in a narrative framework. He introduces the reader to the topic by projecting his subjective state of mind into a persona. It is the latter that tells the story of a failed relationship thus appearing to be infused with the author's emotion.

This is made obvious by the use of personal pronouns like "we" and "us" occurring already in the first line. By dealing with a topic common to most people, the persona not only attracts the reader's attention but also evokes his empathy. Without this feeling, the author would not be able to communicate the emotion of suffering, as it would be a purely intellectual and associative idea. What makes the reader understand and appreciate the subject matter conveyed in the poem is his capacity to experience another's feelings. If the reader did not develop this empathy in the course of the poem, he is almost forced to do so in the last three lines. Here, the triple repetition of the pronoun "my" deeply stirs the reader, making him see the persona's degree of affectedness. In other words, the narrative could be seen as an objective correlative of the universal subject of suffering caused by the conflict between ratio and emotion. The persona's feelings symbolize the emotion the author wants to express, thus evoking an emotional response in the reader. Without the narrative, the poem would simply be an enumeration of facts that do not necessarily affect the reader. In this way, then, it is the narrative framework that immerses the reader into the subject matter.

The language used in the poem is full of imagery. This mostly negative imagery serves the purpose of making the reader perceive the atmosphere of the poem through association with commonly known things and situations. It evolves around the metaphor of a road which stands for the bond that used to connect the lovers. This metaphor appears already in the title and is referred to in every stanza. As the title "No Road" already suggests, the connection between the persona and his former partner has broken down. Having ended their commitment in mutual agreement, they have gone separate ways. The author stresses the finality of this decision by using the metaphoric image "bricked our gates up" (l.2). This image of deterioration stands for the shutting down of any possibilities of communication, which is again stressed by the image of the creation of a natural barrier between the former lovers ("planted trees to screen us" l.2). The picture created especially by the first picture is a very sad and desolate one. Whenever entrances are sealed, it means that there is no hope for recovery. Bricking up doors is the final action when a building is being closed down permanently.

This gloomy atmosphere created already in the metaphorical title and the first stanza is brightened by the image introducing the second stanza. Here, the author pictures a decaying garden that has been neglected to emphasize the persona's hope of not losing his partner. Even though the scene that is being portrayed is that of neglect and decay ("leaves drift unswept", "grass creeps unmown" l.7), it also conveys a feeling of hope as the current state could still be revoked. The same way as it is not too late to save the garden if it is looked after again ("so little overgrown" l.9), the former lovers' relationship could be as it was before their separation. The road mentioned before is still open but it will break down eventually if no measures are taken against the process of deterioration. The last stanza depicts a gloomy view of a future in which the connection between the persona and his former partner has broken down completely. Here again, the author uses the negative metaphor "no road" (l.13) to underline the persona's final loss of his partner. The recurring use of this metaphorical image stresses that the idea of losing that person seems unbearable for the speaker. It also makes the reader picture the situation and actually realize its gravity. To put it in a nutshell, one of the main devices used to vividly illustrate the meaning of the poem is imagery.

The persona portrays the world without his partner in the paradoxical simile "like a cold sun" (l.15). By comparing two essentially unlike things the author draws the reader's attention to this contrast, making it extremely graphic to him. No one can survive without the power of the sun. If it stopped shining all creatures on earth would be doomed to extinction. Like every living creature depends on the warmth of the sun, without which life is not possible, the persona cannot live without his partner. He feels that if he cannot be with him, there is no reason for him to survive as it would only mean endless suffering. Despite this, he hesitates to make a decision. The final position of this stylistic device in the poem suggests that he has already given up. Even though he knows he is facing enormous pain, it seems that any other decision would not ease his suffering. He prefers to choose a way which he has got a clear picture of, as the elaborate simile shows. It might be painful, but at least he knows what to expect. In this way, it is this simile that not only communicates the subject matter but also makes it graphic for the reader.

An important element the author uses to express the topic of the poem is alliteration. The harsh sounding alliteration "planted trees to [...] turned all time's" (ll.3-4) underlines the efforts made by both partners to put distance between them. The triple occurrence of the plosive "t" not only interrupts the air stream in the mouth abruptly, but by doing so, it also disrupts the rhythm of the poem. The recurrence of this voiceless consonant emphasizes how difficult it was for the persona and his former partner to let go and how hard they have tried. This is also expressed by the alliteration "Silence, and space, and strangers" (l.5) embedded in a polysyndeton. Here, the use of sibilants speeds up the rhythm of a poem, thus stressing the enumeration that emphasizes their active attempts to break the bond between them. The alliterations used in the second stanza have a calming effect. By having the persona use several soft-sounding, soothing alliterations (l.9, l.10, l.11), the author gives the impression that there is still hope for him and his partner. It seems that it is not too late to retrace their steps. On the other hand, the repetition of these sounds suggests the persona's desperation which causes him to cling to the old times. As his fear of being alone and the pain caused by the separation become stronger, he tries to tranquilize himself. This feeling of despair reaches a climax in the last stanza. It seems that the persona is helpless in his situation. The alliteration "world where no such road will run" (l.13) again speeds up the rhythm of the poem stressing that time is running out. Even so, he does not know how to decide. Instead, he stays passive as the alliteration "watch that world" (l.15) shows. He knows that he should not lose any time, but after having thought the situation through, he has abandoned any hopes and given in to the suffering. In this way, then, it is the use of alliteration that stresses the meaning of the poem.

A further device used to communicate the idea the author wants to express via his poem is enjambment. Only six out of eighteen lines in the poem are connected by run-on lines. The enjambments could stand for the letting-go of the feelings, whereas the end-stopped lines seem to reflect containment. It seems as if despite his emotions the persona was trying to be as contained and rational as possible. This conflict between reason and emotion starts already in the first stanza.

Whereas in the first line the persona is overwhelmed by his feelings, he manages to pull himself together in the next three lines, but eventually needs to allow his emotions to flow. In those moments of weakness, the pain is too strong. The use of exclusively end-stopped lines in the second stanza not only underlines the persona's effort to hold back his emotions, but also introduces a feeling of hope replacing the intense suffering. Even though he realizes that time is running out, he still sees a chance for them to get back together. At the same time, the enjambment in the first line of the last stanza depicts the persona's shattered hopes. The more he thinks about his lost love the less hopeful he is to win his partner back. Thus, the two lines linked by the run-on line are an exclamation of pain he can no longer control. After this, he goes over to a rational view of the situation. These last lines are end-stopped; the punctuation limiting them seems like a metaphor of the control he is exercising to remain rational. To sum up, one of the main devices to communicate the essence of the poem is enjambment.

It is also the use of litotes that plays an important role for the reader's understanding of the poet's intention. This device, which in this poem occurs in the last stanza ("Not to prevent" l. 17), is embedded in several other stylistic means supporting it. The use of a double negation again emphasizes the persona's inner conflict. Although his biggest desire is to avert the final breakdown of his relationship, he denies himself this wish for reasons that remain unknown to the reader. What adds to the gravity of his pseudo-conclusion is its arrangement in the poem. The fact that it appears in final position means that it is the persona's last resort after having considered the situation intensely. Even though the last lines are very elaborate and show a high degree of containment, the focus position of what seems to be the persona's last will expresses his desperation. His inner conflict causes him endless suffering from which he cannot escape. All in all, it is the use of litotes that expresses the poet's intention.

Summing up, the central topic of the poem is the eternal human conflict between reason and emotion. Both the narrative and the stylistic devices such as imagery, simile, alliteration, enjambment, and litotes communicate and underline this message.

The first intends to evoke the reader's empathy with the persona's situation. It can also be seen as an objective correlative of the universal subject of suffering caused by the conflict mentioned. The latter, on the other hand, has the purpose to stress the message of the poem by supporting the narrative.

YOUR KNOWLEDGE HAS VALUE

- We will publish your bachelor's and master's thesis, essays and papers

- Your own eBook and book - sold worldwide in all relevant shops

- Earn money with each sale

Upload your text at www.GRIN.com
and publish for free